itty-bitty
BIBLE
Activity Book
Old Testament
Volume 7

Warner Press Kids
educate • nurture • inspire

Written by Belinda Mooney • Illustrations by Kevin Spear

CREATION

God created the world in seven days. Match what He made or what He did with the correct day it happened.
You can find the answers in Genesis 1:1—2:3.

Day 1   God rested.

Day 2   He made the birds and the fishes.

Day 3   He made dry land and plants.

Day 4   He made the day and night.

Day 5   He separated the waters and the firmament.

Day 6   He made the sun, moon and stars.

Day 7   God created the animals and man.

Answer on Page 41

GARDEN OF EDEN

God put Adam and Eve in a beautiful garden to live. They didn't have many of the things we have today. Can you find the things in the garden that would not belong there?

Answer on Page 41

Adam and Eve

Circle the correct answer to the following questions. You can find the answers by reading Genesis 3.

1. What animal talked to Eve in the garden?

   Dog   Serpent   Owl

2. Eve said she could eat from every tree but one. Which tree wasn't she supposed to touch?

   Tree of Life   **Tree of Knowledge of Good & Evil**   **Tree of Fun**

3. God told her and Adam something would happen if they did eat from that tree. What was it?

   They would die   They would get old   Nothing

4. Did the serpent agree with God, on what would happen to them?

   Yes   No

5. What kind of fruit did Eve eat from the tree?

   Apples   Grapes   The Bible doesn't say

6. After Eve eats the fruit what does she do next?

   Gives some to Adam   Falls over dead   Sits and has some more

7. After Adam ate some of the fruit they realized they had no clothes on so they got some by...

Going to the store   Making fur clothes   Sewing leaves together

8. Who was looking for Adam as he walked in the garden?

The serpent   God   Eve

9. What was Adam doing that he couldn't be found?

Working   Swimming   Hiding

10. God asks Adam why he ate from the tree. Who does Adam blame for giving him the fruit to eat?

God   Eve   Serpent

11. God curses the serpent for deceiving Adam and Eve. The serpent now must crawl on what?

His belly   His back   All four legs

12. Adam and Eve have to leave their beautiful garden forever and God puts something there to guard it. What does He put?

Snakes   A big gate   Angels and a flaming sword

Answer on Page 41

CAIN AND ABEL

Adam and Eve had two sons, Cain and Abel. When Cain's offering is not accepted by God and Abel's is, Cain gets very mad and kills Abel.

Word search – Find the words from Genesis 4:1–16

N	L	R	A	H	S	L	Q	F	P	C	B	Z	F
O	P	F	P	S	W	R	H	I	U	L	R	M	R
N	O	D	L	N	Z	C	F	E	N	G	O	V	U
B	B	J	L	M	I	V	L	L	I	C	T	Z	I
R	E	V	E	I	J	T	O	D	S	H	H	K	T
R	S	P	G	N	A	A	C	S	H	A	E	N	S
Y	L	M	W	L	X	D	K	G	M	T	R	G	C
M	E	J	S	K	V	A	N	S	E	V	T	Z	A
I	W	P	T	U	Y	M	K	I	N	W	X	O	I
R	A	E	Z	A	B	E	L	P	T	N	N	M	N
P	H	K	O	W	K	O	F	F	E	R	I	N	G
J	R	M	O	K	W	L	A	Z	Q	K	U	Q	L
S	X	O	O	I	I	W	A	G	U	E	U	G	P
V	A	G	A	B	O	N	D	V	P	N	K	U	S

1. Cain	5. offering	9. fruit	13. Nod
2. Abel	6. fields	10. slew	
3. Adam	7. brother	11. punishment	
4. Eve	8. flock	12. vagabond	

Answer on Page 42

CAIN WANDERS

Because he killed his brother Cain had to wander the earth. He eventually built a city.
Help Cain get to the city.

Answer on Page 42

NOAH AND THE FLOOD

God told Noah to take the animals into the Ark in pairs. These were the unclean animals that went in two by two. The clean animals, the ones that they could eat and sacrifice, he took seven of each animal on board the Ark.

Count by two's to see how many of each animal went in the Ark. Write the numbers in order above the letters to make the code. Use the code to see what the names of Noah's sons were.

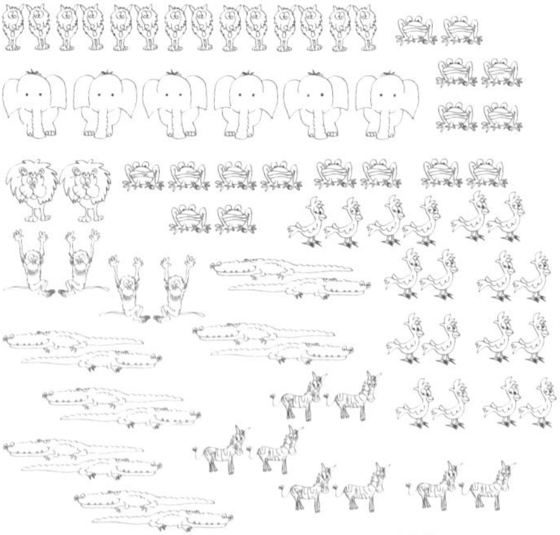

How many dogs? _____ =P

How many elephants ___ =H

How many frogs? _____ =S

How many lions? _____ =A

How many birds? _____ =T

How many monkeys? ___ =E

How many alligators? __ =M

How many zebras? _____ =J

Code Key

	P	H	S	A	T	E	M	J
1.	16	6	4	12				
2.	6	2	12					
3.	8	2	14	6	4	18	6	

Answer on Page 42

8

NOAH AND THE RAINBOW

God put a rainbow in the sky as proof of His promise never to flood the earth again. Color the picture. Give the rainbow lots of different colors.

MAKE YOUR OWN PICTURE

Just for Fun – Paint your own picture. Start with the basic colors and then mix your own.

Start with   **RED   BLUE   YELLOW**

Use these colors to make other colors:

RED & BLUE = PURPLE   RED & YELLOW = ORANGE

BLUE & YELLOW = GREEN

To make lighter colors add some white. To make brown mix a little bit of each color.

TOWER OF BABEL

At first the people of the earth spoke one language. Then the people decided to build a huge tower so they could be powerful like God. God wasn't happy with them so He decided to give them different languages and scatter them all over the world.

How many languages can you say good morning in? Match the phrase with the country it comes from.

1. Good Morning   a. Spain

2. Bonjour   b. Ireland (Celtic)

3. Guten Morgen   c. United States

4. Maidin mhaith dhuit   d. Germany

5. Buongiorno   e. Italy

6. Buenos días   f. France

There are now many countries that speak different languages. Fill in the blanks with the names of the countries.

Across:

United States
(hint: the gray spot is the blank spot in between the two words)

Greece

France

Israel

Ireland

Spain

England

Down:

Canada

Norway

Switzerland

Germany

Australia

Answer on Page 42

ABRAM AND SARAI

Abram and Sarai had to leave the country where they were born to follow the Lord's command. God would give them new names, Abraham and Sarah, and a baby boy when Sarah was too old to have children.

Trace the path Abram & Sarai took to get from Ur to Canaan.

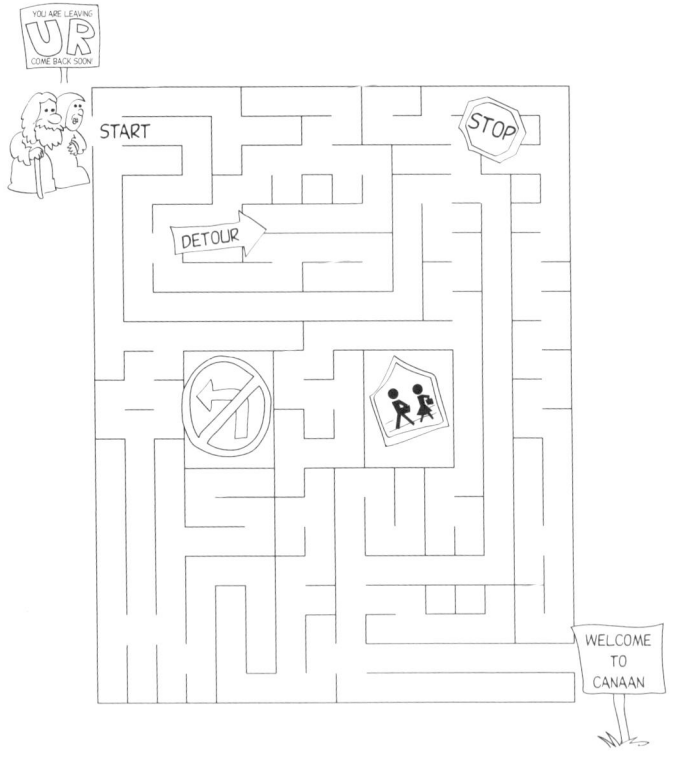

Answer on Page 43

BOOKS OF THE BIBLE

There are 66 books in the whole Bible. There are 39 in the Old Testament. The book of Isaiah is often called the "mini" Bible because it has 66 chapters.

```
X  K  Y  N  F  N  L  A  M  E  N  T  A  T  I  O  N  S
D  Y  I  D  Y  U  E  F  L  C  C  V  P  C  N  U  B  R
A  T  E  S  V  M  I  S  C  B  H  A  I  M  E  H  E  N
Y  L  C  O  H  B  G  R  T  C  O  R  S  U  D  O  X  E
P  E  C  N  V  E  X  E  P  H  P  U  Z  W  L  T  C  M
W  V  L  G  T  R  D  E  U  T  E  R  O  N  O  M  Y  P
O  I  E  O  E  S  I  J  I  K  S  R  D  Z  D  S  S  Z
Y  T  S  F  G  J  G  I  J  F  A  S  Z  W  O  A  F  G
Q  I  I  S  E  E  U  H  O  T  M  B  O  J  L  R  D  K
E  C  A  O  X  K  N  D  W  V  U  J  A  M  U  I  B  D
Q  U  S  L  E  J  G  E  G  P  E  O  S  T  Z  K  W  S
Q  S  T  O  W  F  M  K  S  E  L  X  H  R  V  H  F  T
U  L  I  M  V  X  I  B  W  I  S  M  R  R  Q  S  E  E
H  L  E  O  A  N  H  A  U  H  S  O  J  G  O  Q  Z  S
N  A  S  N  G  C  H  R  O  N  I  C  L  E  S  R  I  E
W  N  O  S  B  R  E  V  O  R  P  Y  N  P  A  W  U  L
```

1. Genesis	6. Joshua	11. Ezra	16. Psalms
2. Exodus	7. Judges	12. Nehemiah	17. Proverbs
3. Leviticus	8. Ruth	13. Kings	18. Ecclesiasties
4. Numbers	9. Samuel	14. Esther	19. Song of Solomon
5. Deuteronomy	10. Chronicles	15. Job	20. Lamentations

Answer on Page 43

JACOB'S LADDER

Jacob has a dream where he sees angels going up a ladder. God speaks to him in this dream and tells Jacob He will always be with him.

Read the verses below. Unscramble the words on the ladder to complete the sentences.

RADDEME

LDEDRA

AEEHNV

ASNLGE

DGO

AEFHTR

EEDS

And he _ _ _ _ _ _ _ _, and behold a _ _ _ _ _ _ set up on the earth, and the top of it reached to _ _ _ _ _ _ _: and behold the _ _ _ _ _ _ of God ascending and descending on it. And, behold, the LORD stood above it, and said, I am the LORD _ _ _ of Abraham thy _ _ _ _ _ _ _, and the God of Isaac: the land whereon thou liest, to thee will I give it, and to thy _ _ _ _ . Genesis 28:12-13

Answer on Page 43

JOSEPH

Jacob had a large family. He had twelve sons but Joseph was the most special of them all to him. He gave Joseph a coat of many colors to show how much he loved him.

Color the picture of Joseph in his new coat.

BABY IN A BASKET

Pharaoh ordered all the baby boys of the Israelite slaves to be killed. So Moses' mother hid him in a basket and sent him down the river. Pharaoh's daughter found him and raised him as her own.

Help Pharaoh's daughter get to the baby in the basket. Can you find Moses' sister hiding in the bushes watching over him?

Answer on Page 43

LET MY PEOPLE GO

When Moses went back to free his people from the Egyptians, Pharaoh refused to let the people go. So God sent ten plagues to Egypt. Finally after the last one Pharaoh told Moses to take the people and go.

Read the verses and fill in the blanks to see what the plagues were.

1. All the water and rivers were turned to _____ (Exodus 7:20)

2. _____ came up out of the waters. (Exodus 8:6)

3. Tiny bugs that bite, called _____ God sent out of the dust. (Exodus 8:16)

4. The Egyptians were attacked by swarms of _____ but the Israelites were protected by God. (Exodus 8:24)

5. God caused all the Egyptian _____ to die. (Exodus 9:6)

6. Moses sprinkled ashes and _____ came on men and animals. These were big, painful sores. (Exodus 9:10)

7. The Lord sent _____ and _____ _____ from the heavens. (Exodus 9:23)

8. The _____ came and ate everything in sight. (Exodus 10:12)

9. _____ covered the land, after Moses stretched forth his hand, for three days. (Exodus 10:22)

10. The last plague was the worst. God sent an angel of death and all the _____ of Egypt were to die. (Exodus 11:5)

Answer on Page 44

THE EXODUS

After Pharaoh set the people free they left Egypt.
Thousands and thousands of Israelites left.
But Pharaoh decided he wanted them back
so he sent his armies out after them. Soon they
were at the shore of the Red Sea with no place
to go, and the chariots close behind them.
What would Moses do?

Cross out every other word to read what
Moses did. Write the answer below.

But when lift see thou from up your thy me rod, so and
go stretch lie out in thine our hand none over under the
it sea ocean, and to divide split it: them and to the many
children people of is Israel Egypt shall use go run on in
dry wet ground dirt through over the was midst bottom
of for the you sea water.

_____

_____

_____

_____

_____

Read Exodus 14:16 to check your answer

Answer on Page 44

THE TEN COMMANDMENTS

God gave Moses the Ten Commandments as rules for His people to live by. They are still important rules for us today.

Read Exodus 20 and number the commandments in the order God gave them to the Israelites.

_____ Thou shalt not bear false witness.

_____ Thou shalt not kill.

_____ Remember the Sabbath day, to keep it holy.

_____ Thou shalt have no other gods before me.

_____ Thou shalt not commit adultery.

_____ Thou shalt not take the name of the Lord thy God in vain.

_____ Thou shalt not make unto thee any graven image.

_____ Thou shalt not covet what is your neighbor's.

_____ Honour thy father and thy mother.

_____ Thou shalt not steal.

Answer on Page 44

THE TWELVE SPIES

Joshua, Caleb and ten other men were sent to spy out the land. Ten of them said they were afraid because of the giants in the land. But not Joshua and Caleb. They knew that if the Lord told them to take the land, He would keep them safe.

Write the beginning letter of the picture to discover what God said would be flowing in the land.

Answer on Page 44

DEBORAH

Deborah was a judge of Israel. When it came time to go into battle, Barak, one of the leaders of the army, did not want to go unless Deborah went with him. Because of this Deborah told him a woman would have the victory.

Do the math problem inside the music note. If the answer is between 1 and 6, color the note blue. If it is between 7 and 10 color it yellow. Now put the letters from the blue notes on the correct number below to find out the name of the enemy who was killed.

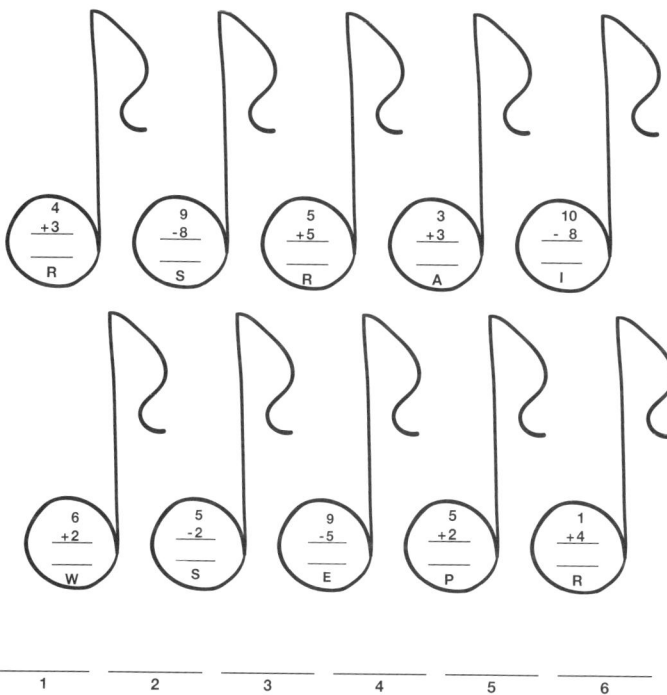

| 1 | 2 | 3 | 4 | 5 | 6 |

Answer on Page 45

SAMSON

Samson had great strength given to him by God. But he didn't obey God and got caught up in sin. He lost his great strength and his enemies blinded him. One day Samson prayed to God to give him back his strength for one last time. God did and Samson pulled the pillars down and destroyed his enemies.

Color the picture of Samson.

RUTH

Ruth was a Moabitess who married a Jewish man. When her husband and father-in-law died, Ruth decided to stay with her mother-in-law Naomi. Ruth loved Naomi very much. They went back to Naomi's hometown where Ruth worked very hard. She married a man named Boaz. Jesus would later come from their family.

Color every third stalk of grain yellow and the others green. Write the yellow letters, in order, on the lines to answer the questions.

Ruth and Boaz had a son. What was his name?

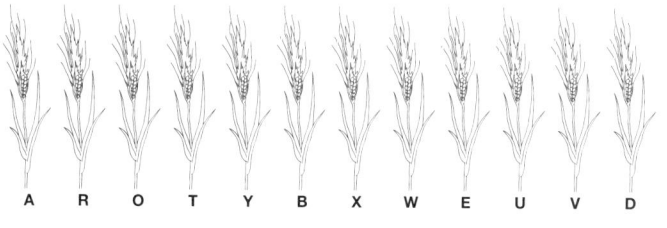

A   R   O   T   Y   B   X   W   E   U   V   D

___   ___   ___   ___

Their son would be grandfather to a famous slayer of giants. What was his name?

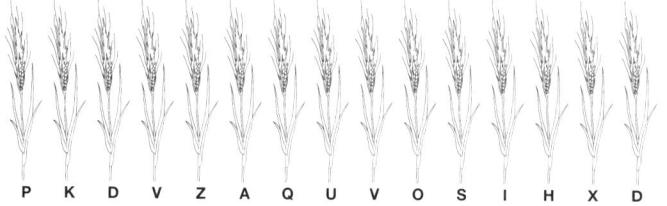

P   K   D   V   Z   A   Q   U   V   O   S   I   H   X   D

___   ___   ___   ___   ___

Answer on Page 45

GOD CALLS SAMUEL

Samuel was asleep when he thought he heard his name called. He looked around and saw no one. He heard it again. He asked Eli the priest what he should do. Eli told him to tell God "Here am I." Samuel listened for God to speak and then gave himself to the Lord. We need to listen to God speak to us through His Word, the Bible.

Can you find the items hidden in Samuel's room? There is an oil lamp, rope, donkey, Bible, and a ladybug.

Answer on Page 45

DAVID AND GOLIATH

David saw that the Israelites were afraid to fight against Goliath. So he took up his sling and some pebbles and went out to fight. God guided his stones and he was able to slay Goliath.

Some of David's stones have fallen out of his bag in a scramble. Can you unscramble them to see what he is trying to spell?

" I _ _ _ _ in the
_ _ _ _ of _ _ _
_ _ _ _ ."

Answer on Page 45

KING DAVID

David later became a great king. The Israelites loved him and God called him a man after His own heart.

Decode the words that tell something about David.

CODE:

A	B	C	D	E	F	G	H	I	J	K	L	M	N	O	P	Q	R	S	T	U	V	W	X	Y	Z
3	14	16	25	12	11	13	20	22	2	8	5	6	9	1	19	21	24	4	7	23	17	26	15	10	18

1. ___ ___ ___ ___   (David killed one of these animals)
   5   22   19   9

2. ___ ___ ___ ___ ___ ___ ___ ___   (This was David's job at home)
   4   20   12   1   20   12   24   25

3. ___ ___ ___ ___   (David became this)
   8   22   9   13

4. ___ ___ ___ ___ ___ ___ ___   (He was attacking the Israelites)
   13   19   5   22   3   7   20

5. ___ ___ ___ ___ ___   (David took care of these)
   4   20   12   12   1

6. ___ ___ ___ ___   (He was king before David)
   4   3   23   5

7. ___ ___ ___ ___   (He played this to soothe Saul)
   20   3   24   1

8. ___ ___ ___ ___ ___ ___   (This prophet anointed David)
   4   3   6   23   12   5

Answer on Page 46

WISDOM OF SOLOMON

Solomon was David's son and became king after David died. God told Solomon he could ask for anything he wanted and God would give it to him. Solomon asked God for wisdom to rule wisely, so God gave him not only wisdom but riches and glory as well.

How many words can you make from these three?

WISDOM OF SOLOMON

SOLOMON'S TEMPLE

David wanted to build a temple for the Lord but God would not let him. His son, Solomon, was to build the temple. He had his men build a magnificent temple for the Lord where the people could worship.

Here are some of the things the temple was built with. See how many you can find.

CODE:

A	B	C	D	E	F	G	H	I	J	K	L	M	N	O	P	Q	R	S	T	U	V	W	X	Y	Z
8	20	10	25	18	23	24	17	2	11	7	6	13	14	16	3	19	1	21	22	15	5	4	12	26	9

1. 16•6•2•5•18 22•1•18•18 _____

2. 20•1•8•21•21 _____

3. 24•16•6•25 _____

4. 10•18•25•8•1 _____

5. 10•26•3•1•18•21•21 _____

6. 21•2•6•5•18•1 _____

7. 23•2•1 _____

8. 21•22•16•14•18•21 _____

9. 2•1•16•14 14•8•2•6•21 _____

Answer on Page 46

QUEEN ESTHER

Esther was Jewish. She was also a queen. When her people, the Israelites, were about to be killed she was willing to risk her life to save them. She trusted in God to protect her and was willing to stand up for God.

We need to be like Esther. Color the crown. Color and cut out the jewels that are good qualities Queen Esther had—ones we should want too. Glue the jewels on the crown.

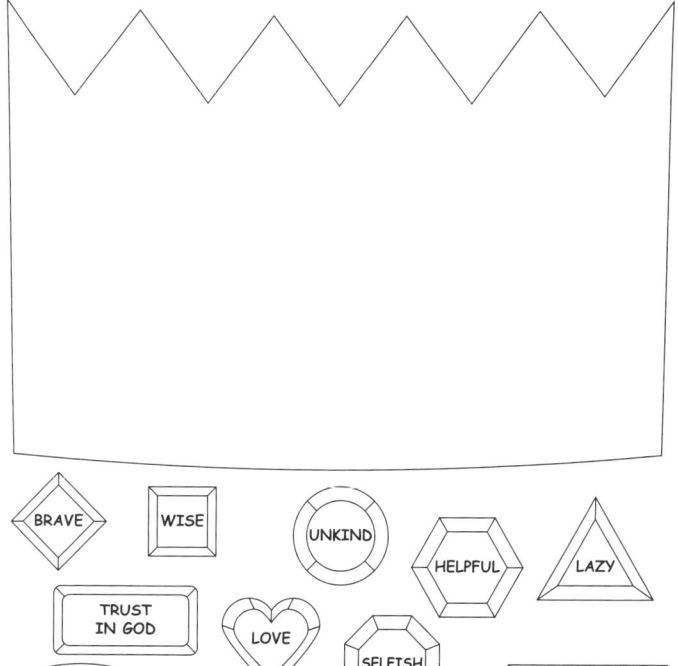

BRAVE

WISE

UNKIND

HELPFUL

LAZY

TRUST IN GOD

LOVE

SELFISH

SELF-CONTROL

WHINING & COMPLAINING

Answer on Page 46

JONAH

God told Jonah to go to Nineveh and tell the people they needed to repent. Jonah did not want to go so he decided to run away. He was on a ship when a big storm came up. Jonah told the sailors to throw him overboard to save themselves. They threw him in and he was swallowed by a large fish. He was in the belly of the fish for three days before it spat him back on dry ground.

What did the city do when Jonah finally preached to them? Use the words in the word bank to complete the verses. You can find the answers in Jonah 3:5.

So the people of _____ believed _____; they proclaimed a _____ and put on _____— from the greatest of _____ even to the _____ of them.

WORD BANK
FAST GOD LEAST NINEVEH SACKCLOTH THEM

Answer on Page 46

OLD TESTAMENT BOOKS OF THE BIBLE

Here are some of the books you can read in the Old Testament. How many can you find in the puzzle?

```
X  K  Y  N  F  N  L  A  M  E  N  T  A  T  I  O  N  S
D  Y  I  D  Y  U  E  F  L  C  C  V  P  C  N  U  B  R
A  T  E  S  V  M  I  S  C  B  H  A  I  M  E  H  E  N
Y  L  C  O  H  B  G  R  T  C  O  R  S  U  D  O  X  E
P  E  C  N  V  E  X  E  P  H  P  U  Z  W  L  T  C  M
W  V  L  G  T  R  D  E  U  T  E  R  O  N  O  M  Y  P
O  I  E  O  E  S  I  J  I  K  S  R  D  Z  D  S  S  Z
Y  T  S  F  G  J  G  I  J  F  A  S  Z  W  O  A  F  G
Q  I  I  S  E  E  U  H  O  T  M  B  O  J  L  R  D  K
E  C  A  O  X  K  N  D  W  V  U  J  A  M  U  I  B  D
Q  U  S  L  E  J  G  E  G  P  E  O  S  T  Z  K  W  S
Q  S  T  O  W  F  M  K  S  E  L  X  H  R  V  H  F  T
U  L  I  M  V  X  I  B  W  I  S  M  R  R  Q  S  E  E
H  L  E  O  A  N  H  A  U  H  S  O  J  G  O  Q  Z  S
N  A  S  N  G  C  H  R  O  N  I  C  L  E  S  R  I  E
W  N  O  S  S  B  R  E  V  O  R  P  N  P  A  W  U  L
```

1. Genesis	6. Joshua	11. Chronicles	16. Psalms
2. Exodus	7. Judges	12. Ezra	17. Proverbs
3. Leviticus	8. Ruth	13. Nehemiah	18. Ecclesiasties
4. Numbers	9. Samuel	14. Esther	19. Song of Solomon
5. Deuteronomy	10. Kings	15. Job	20. Lamentations

Answer on Page 47

DANIEL MAKES A CHOICE

Daniel and his friends were captured by the enemy. Even though they were in the country of the enemy they made right choices. They ate the things God had told them to and upheld His laws. You can make good choices too. Make a list of some things that are good for you to do.

List

DANIEL AND THE LIONS

When Daniel refused to bow down to the king he was thrown in to the lion's den. But God honored Daniel's commitment to Him and shut the lions' mouths.

Complete the dot-to-dot.

Answer on Page 47

ISAIAH

Isaiah was a wise prophet. He told about the coming of the Messiah.

The following verses are all prophecies that told about Jesus long before He was born.

Look up the verses and find the missing words.

Fill in the blanks to finish the prophecies foretold in Isaiah.

1. And he shall _____ among
   the nations, and shall _____
   many people: and they shall beat their
   _____ into plowshares, and their
   _____ into pruning hooks: nation shall
   not lift up sword against _____, neither shall they
   learn _____ anymore. *Isaiah 2:4*

2. Therefore the Lord himself shall give you a _____:
   behold, a _____ shall conceive, and bear a _____,
   and shall call his name _____. *Isaiah 7:14*

3. For unto us a _____ is born, unto us a son is given:
   and the _____ shall be upon his shoulder:
   and his name shall be called _____, Counsellor,
   The _____ God, The everlasting _____,
   The _____ of _____. *Isaiah 9:6*

4. And there shall come forth a _____ out of the stem of
   _____, and a Branch shall grow out of his _____.
   Isaiah 11:1

5. And shall make him of _____ understanding in the
   _____ of the Lord: and he shall not _____ after the
   sight of his _____, neither reprove after the hearing
   of his ears. *Isaiah 11:3*

6. A bruised _____ shall he not _____, and the
   smoking _____ shall he not _____: he shall bring
   forth _____unto truth. *Isaiah 42: 3*

7. Surely he hath borne our _____, and he carried
   our _____: yet we did esteem him _____,
   smitten of God, and afflicted. *Isaiah 53:4*

8. Behold, I have given him for a _____ to the people,
   a _____ and _____ to the people.
   Isaiah 55:4

Answer on Page 47

FIERY FURNACE

Shadrach, Meshach and Abednego were thrown into a fiery furnace but because they had obeyed the Lord, He kept them safe. The king saw another man walking around in the furnace with the men. Who do you think it was?

Here are the names of some men of the Old Testament. Using the code below, find out who they are, then write the letters from the shaded boxes on the blanks to see who was in the fire with the three men.

WHO AM I?

I led an army against Jericho:		☀	🌳	△	🏠	⚗	👑
As a baby I was placed in a basket:		◯	🌳	△	☆	△	
I was once a God-fearing king, but then I disobeyed the Lord:		△	👑	⚗	☾		
My mother gave me back to the Lord—to serve Him:		△	👑	◯	⚗	☆	☾
A couple built a special room on their house just for me:		☆	☾	🔥	△	🏠	👑

Who was in the fire too? ____ ____ ____ ____

CODE									
👑	☆	🏠	🔥	☀	☾	◯	🌳	△	⚗
A	E	H	I	J	L	M	O	S	U

Answer on Page 48

PSALM 23

Color the miniposter. Cut it out and glue it on construction paper. Give it to someone you love.

The LORD is my Shepherd, I shall not be in want.

PROVERBS

In Proverbs God often uses animals as examples of what we should do—such as hard working like the ant—or He gives us a picture of something He is trying to show us—such as sin being like a roaring lion. Read a chapter of Proverbs every day.

Here is a list of some of the animals God mentions in Proverbs. Can you find them in this picture?

hind(deer)   ant   ox   bear   bird   lion   horse   dog
lamb   goat   eagle   serpent   locust(grasshopper)   spider

Answer on Page 48

The Prophets

Here are some more names of God's prophets in the Old Testament. These men preached God's Word even if it meant they would be put to death.

Match the name of the prophet to the shape it fits in to.

1.

5.

2.

6.

3.

7.

4.

8.

1. Haggai	3. Habakkuk	5. Zephaniah	7. Zechariah
2. Malachi	4. Nahum	6. prophet	8. Nehemiah

Answer on Page 48

GOD'S LOVE

The Old Testament tells us the story of God's love for His chosen people. We can read about the many ways God took care of them and protected them even when they did not listen to Him. God loves us today in the same way.

Make a list of some of the ways God has shown His love to you. Don't forget to include everyday things like a house and food.

I know God loves me because...

ANSWERS

CREATION

God created the world in seven days. Match what He made or what He did with the correct day it happened.
You can find the answers in Genesis 1:1—2:3.

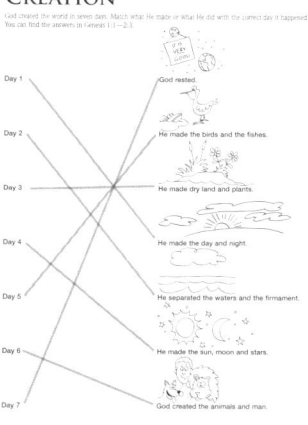

Day 1 — God rested.

Day 2 — He made the birds and the fishes.

Day 3 — He made dry land and plants.

Day 4 — He made the day and night.

Day 5 — He separated the waters and the firmament.

Day 6 — He made the sun, moon and stars.

Day 7 — God created the animals and man.

GARDEN OF EDEN

God put Adam and Eve in a beautiful garden to live. They didn't have many of the things we have today.
Can you find the things in the garden that would not belong there?

ADAM AND EVE

Circle the correct answer to the following questions. You can find the answers by reading Genesis 3.

1. What animal talked to Eve in the garden?
   Dog   (Serpent)   Owl

2. Eve said she could eat from every tree but one. Which tree wasn't she supposed to touch?
   Tree of Life   (Tree of Knowledge of Good & Evil)   Tree of Fun

3. God told her and Adam something would happen if they did eat from that tree. What was it?
   (They would die)   They would get old   Nothing

4. Did the serpent agree with God, on what would happen to them?
   Yes   (No)

5. What kind of fruit did Eve eat from the tree?
   Apples   Grapes   (The Bible doesn't say)

6. After Eve eats the fruit what does she do next?
   (Gives some to Adam)   Falls over dead   Sits and has some more

7. After Adam ate some of the fruit they realized they had no clothes on so they got some by...
   Going to the store   Making fur clothes   (Sewing leaves together)

8. Who was looking for Adam as he walked in the garden?
   The serpent   (God)   Eve

9. What was Adam doing that he couldn't be found?
   Working   Swimming   (Hiding)

10. God asks Adam why he ate from the tree. Who does Adam blame for giving him the fruit to eat?
    God   (Eve)   Serpent

11. God curses the serpent for deceiving Adam and Eve. The serpent now must crawl on what?
    (His belly)   His back   All four legs

12. Adam and Eve have to leave their beautiful garden forever and God puts something there to guard it. What does He put?
    Snakes   A big gate   (Angels and a flaming sword)

ANSWERS

CAIN AND ABEL

Adam and Eve had two sons, Cain and Abel. When Cain's offering is not accepted by God and Abel's is, Cain gets very mad and kills Abel.

Word search - Find the words from Genesis 4:1-16.

N	L	R	A	H	S	L	Q	F	P	C	B	Z	F
O	P	F	P	S	W	R	H	I	U	L	R	M	R
N	O	D	L	N	Z	C	F	E	N	G	O	V	U
B	B	J	L	M	V	I	E	L	I	C	T	T	I
R	E	V	E	I	J	T	O	D	S	H	H	K	T
R	S	P	G	N	A	A	C	S	H	A	E	N	S
Y	L	M	W	L	X	D	K	G	M	T	R	G	C
M	E	J	S	V	A	N	S	E	V	T	O	D	A
I	W	P	T	U	Y	M	K	I	N	W	X	O	I
R	A	E	Z	A	B	E	L	P	H	S	I	N	N
P	H	K	O	W	K	O	F	F	E	R	I	N	G
J	R	M	O	K	W	L	A	Z	Q	K	U	Q	L
S	X	O	O	I	I	W	A	G	U	E	U	G	P
V	A	G	A	B	O	N	D	V	P	N	K	U	S

1. Cain	5. offering	9. fruit	13. Nod
2. Abel	6. fields	10. slew	
3. Adam	7. brother	11. punishment	
4. Eve	8. flock	12. vagabond	

CAIN WANDERS

Because he killed his brother Cain had to wander the earth. He eventually built a city.

Help Cain get to the city.

NOAH AND THE FLOOD

God told Noah to take the animals into the ark in pairs. These were the unclean animals that went in two by two. The clean animals, the ones that they could eat and sacrifice, he took seven of each animal on board the Ark.

Count by two's to see how many of each animal went in the Ark. Write the numbers in order above the letters to make the code. Use the code to see what the names of Noah's sons were.

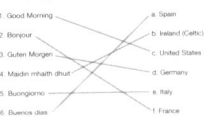

How many dogs? ___14___ =P

How many elephants? ___6___ =H

How many frogs? ___16___ =S

How many lions? ___2___ =A

How many birds? ___18___ =E

How many monkeys? ___4___ =M

How many alligators? ___12___ =M

How many zebras? ___8___ =J

Code Key

14	6	16	2	18	4	12	8
S	H	E	M				
H	A	M					
J	A	P	H	E	T	H	

TOWER OF BABEL

At first the people of the earth spoke one language. Then the people decided to build a huge tower so they could be powerful like God. God wasn't happy with them so He decided to give them different languages and scatter them all over the world.

How many languages can you say good morning in? Match the phrase with the country it comes from.

1. Good Morning — a. Spain
2. Bonjour — b. Ireland (Celtic)
3. Guten Morgen — c. United States
4. Madin mhaith druit — d. Germany
5. Buongiorno — e. Italy
6. Buenos días — f. France

There are now many countries that speak different languages. Fill in the blanks with the names of the countries.

Across:
United States (fill the grey spot in the blank spot in between the two worlds)
Greece
France
Israel
Ireland
Spain
England

Down:
Canada
Norway
Switzerland
Germany
Australia

ANSWERS

ABRAM AND SARAI

Abram and Sarai had to leave the country where they were born to follow the Lord's command. God would give them new names, Abraham and Sarah, and a baby boy when Sarah was too old to have children.

Trace the path Abram & Sarai took to get from Ur to Canaan.

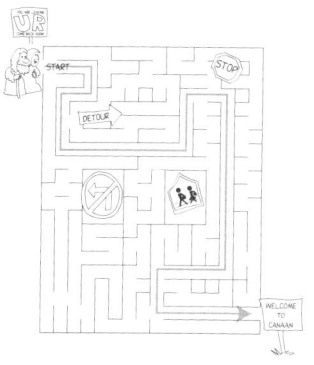

BOOKS OF THE BIBLE

There are 66 books in the whole Bible. There are 39 in the Old Testament. The book of Isaiah is often called the "mini" Bible because it has 66 chapters.

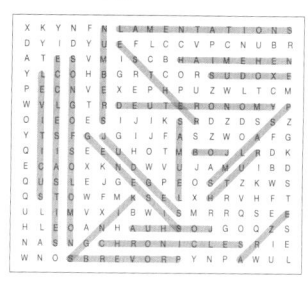

1. Genesis	6. Joshua	11. Ezra	16. Psalms
2. Exodus	7. Judges	12. Nehemiah	17. Proverbs
3. Leviticus	8. Ruth	13. Kings	18. Ecclesiastes
4. Numbers	9. Samuel	14. Father	19. Song of Solomon
5. Deuteronomy	10. Chronicles	15. Job	20. Lamentations

JACOB'S LADDER

And he **DREAMED,** and behold a **LADDER** set up on the earth, and the top of it reached to **HEAVEN**: and behold the **ANGELS** of God ascending and descending on it. And, behold, the LORD stood above it, and said, I *am* the LORD **GOD** of Abraham thy **FATHER**, and the God of Isaac: the land whereon thou liest, to thee will I give it, and to thy **SEED**. Genesis 28:12-13

BABY IN A BASKET

Pharaoh ordered all the baby boys of the Israelite slaves to be killed. So Moses' mother hid him in a basket and sent him down the river. Pharaoh's daughter found him and raised him as her own.

Help Pharaoh get to the babe in the basket. Can you find Moses' sister hiding in the bushes watching over him?

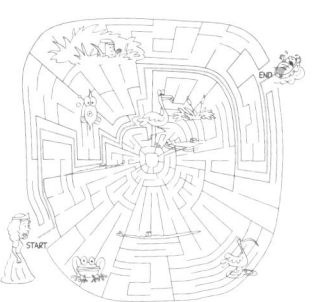

ANSWERS

LET MY PEOPLE GO

When Moses went back to free his people from the Egyptians, Pharaoh refused to let the people go. So God sent ten plagues to Egypt. Finally after the last one Pharaoh told Moses to take the people and go.

Read the verses and fill in the blanks to see what the plagues were.

1. All the water and rivers were turned to **BLOOD** (Exodus 7:20)

2. **FROGS** came up out of the waters. (Exodus 8:6)

3. Tiny bugs that bite, called **LICE** God sent out of the dust. (Exodus 8:16)

4. The Egyptians were attacked by swarms of **FLIES** but the Israelites were protected by God. (Exodus 8:24)

5. God caused all the Egyptian **CATTLE** to die. (Exodus 9:6)

6. Moses sprinkled ashes and **BOILS** came on men and animals. These were big, painful sores. (Exodus 9:10)

7. The Lord sent **THUNDER** and **HAIL** from the heavens. (Exodus 9:23)

8. The **LOCUSTS** came and ate everything in sight. (Exodus 10:12)

9. **DARKNESS** covered the land, after Moses stretched forth his hand, for three days. (Exodus 10:22)

10. The last plague was the worst: God sent an angel of death and all the **FIRSTBORN** of Egypt were to die. (Exodus 11:5)

THE EXODUS

After Pharaoh let the people free they left Egypt. Thousands and thousands of Israelites left. But Pharaoh decided he wanted them back so he sent his armies out after them. Soon they were at the shore of the Red Sea with no place to go, and the chariots close behind them. What would Moses do?

Cross out every other word to read what Moses did. Write the answer below.

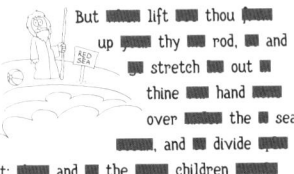

But ~~the~~ lift ~~up~~ thou ~~the~~ up ~~the~~ thy rod, ~~in~~ and ~~up~~ stretch ~~the~~ out ~~the~~ thine ~~the~~ hand ~~the~~ over ~~the~~ the ~~in~~ sea ~~the~~, and ~~in~~ divide it: ~~the~~ and ~~up~~ the ~~the~~ children ~~the~~ of ~~in~~ Israel ~~the~~ shall ~~the~~ go ~~the~~ on dry ~~the~~ ground ~~the~~ through ~~the~~ the ~~the~~ midst ~~the~~ of ~~the~~ the ~~the~~ sea ~~the~~.

But lift thou up they rod and stretch out thine hand over the sea and divide it: and the children of Israel shall go on dry ground through the midst of the sea.

Read Exodus 14:16 to check your answer

THE TEN COMMANDMENTS

God gave Moses the Ten Commandments as rules for his people to live by. They are still important rules for us today.

Read Exodus 20 and number the commandments in the order God gave them to the Israelites.

9 — Thou shalt not bear false witness.

6 — Thou shalt not kill.

4 — Remember the Sabbath day, to keep it holy.

1 — Thou shalt have no other gods before me.

7 — Thou shalt not commit adultery.

3 — Thou shalt not take the name of the LORD thy God in vain.

2 — Thou shalt not make unto thee any graven image.

10 — Thou shalt not covet what is your neighbors.

5 — Honour thy father and thy mother

8 — Thou shalt not steal.

THE TWELVE SPIES

Joshua, Caleb and ten other men were sent to spy out the land. Ten of them said they were afraid because of the giants in the land. But not Joshua and Caleb. They knew that if the Lord told them to take the land, He would keep them safe.

Write the beginning letter of the picture to discover what God said would be flowing in the land.

ANSWERS

DEBORAH

Deborah was a judge of Israel. When it came time to go into battle, Barak, one of the leaders of the army, did not want to go unless Deborah went with him. Because of this Deborah told him a woman would have the victory.

And it was so. The enemy leader fell asleep in a tent and a woman killed him. The Israelites had a victory and Deborah then sang a song of praise to the Lord.

Do the math problem inside the music note. If the answer is between 1 and 6, color the note blue. If it is between 7 and 10 color it yellow. Now put the letters from the blue notes on the correct number below to find out the name of the enemy who was killed.

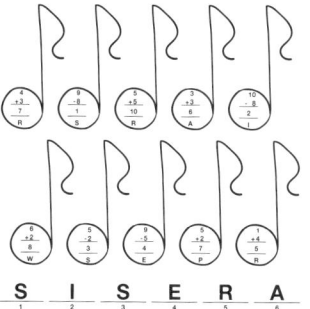

S I S E R A
1 2 3 4 5 6

RUTH

Ruth was a Moabitess who married a Jewish man. When her husband and father-in-law died, Ruth decided to stay with her mother-in-law Naomi. Ruth loved Naomi very much. They went back to Naomi's hometown where Ruth worked very hard. She married a man named Boaz. Jesus would later come from their family.

Color every third stalk of grain yellow and the others green. Write the yellow letters, in order, on the lines to answer the questions.

Ruth and Boaz had a son. What was his name?

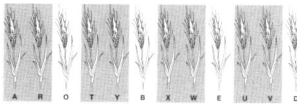

A R O T Y B X W E U V D

OBED

Their son would be grandfather to a famous slayer of giants. What was his name?

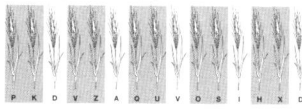

P K D V Z A Q U V O S I H X D

D A V I D

GOD CALLS SAMUEL

Samuel was asleep when he thought he heard his name called. He looked around and saw no one. He heard it again. He asked Eli the priest what he should do. Eli told him to tell God "Here am I." Samuel listened for God to speak and then gave himself to the Lord. We need to listen to God speak to us through His Word, the Bible.

Can you find the items hidden in Samuel's room? There is an oil lamp, rope, donkey, Bible, and a ladybug.

DAVID AND GOLIATH

David saw that the Israelites were afraid to fight against Goliath. So he took up his sling and some pebbles and went out to fight. God guided his stones and he was able to slay Goliath.

Some of David's stones have fallen out of his bag in a scramble. Can you unscramble them to see what he is trying to spell?

ANSWERS

KING DAVID

David later became a great king. The Israelites loved him and God called him a man after His own heart.
Decode the words that tell something about David.

CODE:

A	B	C	D	E	F	G	H	I	J	K	L	M	N	O	P	Q	R	S	T	U	V	W	X	Y	Z
5	14	18	25	12	1	13	19	22	2	6	9	8	10	3	24	16	7	4	21	15	17	23	11	20	16

1. L I D N   (David killed one of these animals)
   9 22 19 9

2. S H E P H E R D   (This was David's job at home)
   4 20 12 1 20 12 24 25

3. K I N G   (David became this)
   6 22 9 13

4. G O L I A T H   (He was attacking the Israelites)
   13 19 5 22 3 7 20

5. S H E E P   (David took care of these)
   4 20 12 12 1

6. S A U L   (He was king before David)
   4 5 15 9

7. H A R P   (He played this to soothe Saul)
   20 3 24 1

8. S A M U E L   (This prophet anointed David)
   4 5 8 23 12 9

SOLOMON'S TEMPLE

David wanted to build a temple for the Lord but God would not let him. His son, Solomon, was to build the temple. He had his men build a magnificent temple for the Lord where the people could worship.

Here are some of the things the temple was built with. See how many you can find.

CODE:

A	B	C	D	E	F	G	H	I	J	K	L	M	N	O	P	Q	R	S	T	U	V	W	X	Y	Z
8	10	18	20	24	22	1	7	2	14	6	4	13	3	19	11	21	22	15	4	12	9	5

1. OLIVE TREE
2. BRASS
3. GOLD
4. CEDAR
5. CYPRESS
6. SILVER
7. FIR
8. STONES
9. IRON NAILS

QUEEN ESTHER

Esther was Jewish. She was also a queen. When her people, the Israelites, were about to be killed she was willing to risk her life to save them. She trusted in God to protect her and was willing to stand up for God.

We need to be like Esther. Color the crown. Color and cut out the words that are **good** qualities Queen Esther had—ones we should want too. Glue the jewels on the crown.

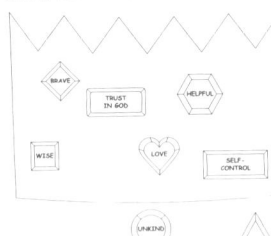

(Placement will vary)

JONAH

God told Jonah to go to Nineveh and tell the people they needed to repent. Jonah did not want to go so he decided to run away. He was on a ship when a big storm came up. Jonah told the sailors to throw him overboard to save themselves. They threw him in and he was swallowed by a large fish. He was in the belly of the fish for three days before it spat him back on dry ground.

What did the city do when Jonah finally preached to them? Use the words in the word bank to complete the verses. You can find the answers in Jonah 3:5.

So the people of <u>NINEVEH</u> believed <u>GOD</u> ; they proclaimed a <u>FAST</u> and put on <u>SACKCLOTH</u> —from the greatest of <u>THEM</u> even to the <u>LEAST</u> of them.

WORD BANK

FAST   GOD   LEAST   NINEVEH   SACKCLOTH   THEM

ANSWERS

OLD TESTAMENT BOOKS OF THE BIBLE

Here are some of the books you can read in the Old Testament. How many can you find in the puzzle?

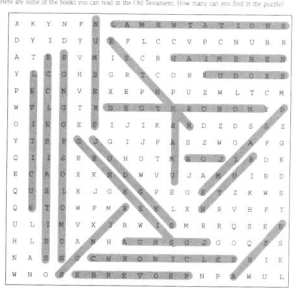

X	K	Y	N	F	R	A	M	E	N	T	A	T	I	O	N	S
D	Y	I	D	Y	U	F	L	C	C	V	P	C	N	U	B
A	T	I	V	K	I	C	R	A	I	H	H	E	R	E	
T	R	A	O	N	G	S	C	O	R	U	B	O	X	E	
P	C	N	V	E	X	F	P	U	Z	W	L	T	C	M	
W	L	G	T	M	E	S	S	H	Q	O	K	O	M		
O	J	E	G	E	I	J	I	K	I	D	Z	S	Z		
Y	T	R	B	G	I	J	F	A	S	Z	W	O	N	P	G
Q	I	K	X	D	H	O	T	R	O	T	Z	A	J		
E	C	A	X	F	M	V	I	J	A	E	I	D	B	O	
Q	U	R	K	J	G	P	E	O	Z	K	W	S			
O	T	O	W	F	M	A	L	X	R	V	H	F	T		
U	L	I	M	V	X	B	W	I	M	R	R	Q	S	K	
H	L	E	G	A	B	I	N	F	M	M	A	Q	O	Q	
N	A	I	C	H	R	O	N	I	C	L	E	S	X	I	E
W	N	O	S	R	K	V	O	K	P	N	P	W	U	L	

1. Genesis	6. Joshua	11. Chronicles	16. Psalms
2. Exodus	7. Judges	12. Ezra	17. Proverbs
3. Leviticus	8. Ruth	13. Nehemiah	18. Ecclesiastes
4. Numbers	9. Samuel	14. Esther	19. Song of Solomon
5. Deuteronomy	10. Kings	15. Job	20. Lamentations

DANIEL AND THE LIONS

When Daniel refused to bow down to the king he was thrown in to the lion's den. But God honored Daniel's commitment to Him and shut the lions' mouths.

Complete the dot-to-dot.

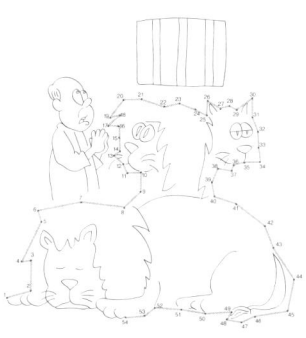

ISAIAH

Isaiah was a wise prophet. He told about the coming of the Messiah.

The following verses are all prophecies that told about Jesus long before he was born.

Look up the verses and find the missing words.

Fill in the blanks to finish the prophecies foretold in Isaiah.

1. And he shall __JUDGE__ among the nations, and shall __REBUKE__ many people: and they shall beat their __SWORDS__ into plowshares, and their __SPEARS__ into pruning hooks: nation shall not lift up sword against __NATION__, neither shall they learn __WAR__ anymore. Isaiah 2:4

2. Therefore the Lord himself shall give you a __SIGN__; behold, a __VIRGIN__ shall conceive, and bear a __SON__, and shall call his name __IMMANUEL__. Isaiah 7:14

3. For unto us a __CHILD__ is born, unto us a son is given: and the __GOVERNMENT__ shall be upon his shoulder: and his name shall be called __WONDERFUL__, Counsellor, The __MIGHTY__ God, The everlasting __FATHER__, The __PRINCE__ of __PEACE__. Isaiah 9:6

4. And there shall come forth a __ROD__ out of the stem of __JESSE__, and a Branch shall grow out of his __ROOTS__. Isaiah 11:1

5. And shall make him of __QUICK__ understanding in the __FEAR__ of the Lord: and he shall not __JUDGE__ after the sight of his __EYES__, neither reprove after the hearing of his ears. Isaiah 11:3

6. A bruised __REED__ shall he not __BREAK__, and the smoking __FLAX__ shall he not __QUENCH__: he shall bring forth __JUDGMENT__ unto truth. Isaiah 42: 3

7. Surely he hath borne our __GRIEFS__, and he carried our __SORROWS__; yet we did esteem him __STRICKEN__, smitten of God, and afflicted. Isaiah 53:4

8. Behold, I have given him for a __WITNESS__ to the people, a __LEADER__ and __COMMANDER__ to the people. Isaiah 55:4

ANSWERS

FIERY FURNACE

Shadrach, Meshach and Abednego were thrown into a fiery furnace but because they had obeyed the Lord, He kept them safe. The king saw another man walking around in the furnace with the men. Who do you think it was?

Here are the names of some men of the Old Testament. Using the code below, find out who they are, then write the letters from the shaded boxes on the blanks to see who was in the fire with the three men.

WHO AM I?

	J	O	S	H	U	A
I led an army against Jericho.	☆	⚱	⌂	♨	◠	△

	M	O	S	E	S	
As a baby I was placed in a basket.	○	⚱	♔	★	⌂	

	S	A	U	L		
I was once a God fearing king, but then I disobeyed the Lord.	⌂	△	◠	☾		

	S	A	M	U	E	L
My mother gave me back to the Lord to serve Him.	⌂	△	○	◠	★	☾

	E	L	I	S	H	A
A couple had a special room on their house just for me.	★	☾	🔥	⌂	♨	△

Who was in the fire too?   **J   E   S   U   S**

CODE										
♔	★	♨	⌂	🔥	☀	☾	⚱	○	△	⊚
A	E	H	I	J	L	M	O	S	U	

THE PROPHETS

Here are some more names of God's prophets in the Old Testament. These men preached God's Word even if it meant they would be put to death.

Match the name of the prophet to the shape it fits in to.

1 prophet

2 Habakkuk

3 Nahum

4 Zephaniah

5 Malachi

6 Zechariah

7 Nehemiah

8 Haggai

1. Haggai	4. Nahum	7. Zechariah
2. Malachi	5. Zephaniah	8. Nehemiah
3. Habakkuk	6. prophet	

PROVERBS

In Proverbs God often uses animals as examples of what we should do—such as hard working like the ant—or He gives us a picture of something He is trying to show us—such as sin being like a roaring lion. Read a chapter of Proverbs every day.

Here is a list of some of the animals God mentions in Proverbs. Can you find them in this picture?

hind (deer)   ant   ox   bear   bird   lion   horse   dog
lamb   goat   eagle   serpent   locust(grasshopper)   spider